Fresh Peaches, Fireworks, & Guns

For Dr. Pafford,
  with all best wishes —
    Don

Fresh Peaches,
Fireworks,
&
Guns

Donald Platt

PURDUE UNIVERSITY PRESS / WEST LAFAYETTE, INDIANA

The paper used in this book meets the minimum requirements of American National Standard for Information Sciences—Permanence of Paper for Printed Library Materials, ANSI Z39.48-1984.

Printed in the United States of America
Design by Chiquita Babb

Thanks to the editors of the following publications where these poems, sometimes in different form, first appeared: *Ironwood:* "Along an Abandoned Spur of the C&O Line," "The Gideon Bible," "Master of the Large Foreheads"; *The Nation:* "Fresh Peaches, Fireworks, & Guns"; *The Paris Review:* "How Night Comes"; *Patchwork Quilts:* "Grandmother's Quilts"; *Poetry:* "Aria for This Listening Area," "Kore"; *Poetry Northwest:* "Along Magnolia St.," "Blackout," "Carolina Steel Co. Canticle," "Counting Vertebrae," "Heliotrope," "Inventing Water," "My Brother Learns to Eat," "Short Mass for My Grandfather," "20/20 Vision," "Untitled"; *Timbuktu:* "April's Algebra," "Grief"; *TriQuarterly:* "My Father's Crucifix"; *The Virginia Quarterly Review:* "Psalm for the Summer Solstice," "Welcome Hardings' Clocks & Music Boxes"; *Weber Studies:* "Life Class," "My High School's Roll of Honor for Its War Dead."

I am indebted to the University of Virginia, Lynchburg College, the Virginia Commission for the Arts, the Virginia Center for the Creative Arts at Sweet Briar, and the University of Utah for various fellowships and grants that aided in the completion of this book. I would like to thank my teachers Charles Wright, Gregory Orr, Jacqueline Osherow, Larry Levis, and Mark Strand for their support and criticism. During the writing of these poems, I received invaluable help from Jill Gonet, Alexander Thorburn, Dana Roeser, and especially Keith Smith. Thanks also to Eavan Boland and Barry Weller for their suggestions on the final version of this manuscript.

Library of Congress Cataloging-in-Publication Data

Platt, Donald, 1957–
    Fresh peaches, fireworks, & guns / Donald Platt.
        p.   cm.
   ISBN 1-55753-048-3
    I. Title. II. Title: Fresh peaches, fireworks, and guns.
PS3566.L286F73 1994
811'.54—DC20   93-40660
                            CIP

CONTENTS

for Dana and Eleanor

FRESH PEACHES, FIREWORKS, & GUNS

Mozart once said that he wrote music
        by finding the notes
that love one another and putting them

        together. But remembering how
the dissonant opening bars of his string quartet
        in C major grate

against each other and yet somehow cohere,
        I like to think
he found a different kind of order,

        the same principle
of musical composition that inspired the roadside sign
        I saw on Rt. 29:

Fresh Peaches, Fireworks, & Guns.
        It makes me do a U-
turn, pull over, and park among the rusted-out

        pick-ups. Here,
under a striped awning, are pyramids of peaches,
        "all local grown,"

the proprietor explains in a drawl whose vowels
        almost drool
peach juice. Next to the flesh

of that fruit ripened
to the color of sunset, shine the blue-black double barrels
of 12-gauge shotguns

and rows of brass shells. For sale, fresh peaches
and slide-action Remingtons,
tempered steel and bruisable fruit, a collision/

collusion that makes
me feel suddenly fragile, a dissonance as pure
as Mozart's, two notes

never put together until now and now forever
inextricable.
After filling a paper bag with peaches, I walk

to the rack of fireworks,
Roman candles, smoke bombs, firecrackers, sparklers
and the ones imported from China

with names like Colorful Bird, Ground Blossom Flower,
and Plum Flowers Report Spring.
There is even a firework called Happiness.

I buy them
for their names, imagine setting them off in celebration
of nothing but their own

tailfeathers of shooting sparks, peony petals of light
opening and exploding,
then falling in a slow divertimento to the ground.

My head full of fireworks,
I pay for them and walk back to my car
in the breathless midsummer

heat, walk back to a world where road dust
has settled like talcum powder
over everything, over the pokeweed and trees of heaven,

over the gas pumps
and out-of-order Coke machine, over the mimosa
with its spike blossoms,

pink sparklers the tree holds in its hundred hands.
Dust has sugared
the battered bodies of the parked trucks

where, on a rear window,
someone has scrawled in a child's block letters
with a forefinger:

JESUS LOVES EVERYBODY EVEN NIGGERS.
Biting into a peach
I let its sweetness fill my mouth. Mozart,

there is no music
for this moment. I have only the taste
of peach juice mixed

with the grit of words I can't spit out,
nigger, 12-gauge,
Georgia, Jesus, poontang, Ground Blossom Flower,

all these gutturals
grinding against each other as if words were stones
under a stutterer's

tongue, which keeps on stumbling over each syllable
until silence,
our final sentence, be said.

ARIA FOR THIS LISTENING AREA

                    Turn the dial,
        voices spill
                    like mercury,
        fill and brim
                    the empty ear's
        semicircular
                    cisterns: scattered
        showers, the best
                    in used cars,
        grand opera, pop,
                    and punk rock,
        talk shows
                    on UFO's,
        crank calls,
                    "Unless you die
        and are born again
                    you shall not enter
        my kingdom,"
                    Local Wheat-Growers
        Mutual Hail
                    and Life Insurance,
        low premiums,
                    another love song,
        aluminum siding,
                    all scrambled in
        one listening area.

                    What poetry!
        This radio,
                    whose dial you spin

until you find

        a frequency

on which the soul

            sings *a cappella*

or plays calypso

           with wooden mallets

on marimbas

        and steel drums.

Are poets only

          deadbeat DJ's

doing time

        on the night shift,

those virtuosos

         of ventriloquism,

their programs mostly

            prerecorded?

Impromptu talkers

         stalk

the wavelengths

        for invisible

listeners.

      What aria

for an area

       with insomnia?

I love any

     area

that "listens."

       How many

pairs of ears

           per square mile

in North Dakota?

              Who else tunes

into this station

           and hears

Heartbreak Hotel

           go out

to Mary Lee

           from Stormin' Norman

at 4 A.M.?

           Language, not

geography,

           is where we live.

Tennessee's

           a way of talking.

I listen for

           the idioms

that mean I'm home,

           a neighbor

saying, "He's not

           wrapped tight,"

or "She's

           a couple

of sandwiches

           short of a picnic,"

or "You're whining

           like a dog

shitting
        persimmon seeds."

Can we map
        a dialect
the way we can
        the Appalachians,
this landslide
        of syllables
that never ends,
        or is speech more
a river that loves
        switching beds
in a flash flood?

        In my split-
level duplex,
        the man who lives
above me keeps
        his blinds down
and TV tuned
        to game shows,
soaps, reruns
        of Guiding Light,
Di-Gel, mouthwash,
        the evening news
"Mass murderer loose
        in Arkansas
celebrates Christmas,

kills his wife
and seven children,"
then sitcoms, Wheel
of Fortune, weather,
whatever plays
the airwaves
at five hundred sixty
megacycles
near the end
of our broadcast day.
Because my neighbor's
hard of hearing
and his floor is my ceiling,
what seeps down,
in the small hours
when I cannot sleep,
is the restless world's
raw nerves,
an insomniac's static,
the monotone
of loneliness.

KORE

This fifth-century B.C. girl
           dressed in flimsy marble,
chiffon of fluted stone,
           whose breasts nuzzle
through transparent folds
           like the noses of deer
as they graze the first yellowy green
           shoots of grass
and lift their heads
           nostrils quivering
to catch the scent of the downwind
           hunter,
is not more beautiful
           than the woman
who got on the subway
           at Symphony
two stops before the museum
           and rode swaying
with her lover to the bump
           and grind of the train,
until someone got off
           and she sat down
with all her classical
           cornucopian curves
and, as he stood next
           to her in the crush
of people, put
           her hand on the inside
of his thigh as if
           they were perfectly
alone and needed

to say nothing more,
her hair combed back
       from her forehead
bound with a woven fillet
       like that of this marble girl
who has survived
       Western civilization,
two and a half thousand years
       of drought, war,
rape and famine,
       her body's long lean note
held on the breath
       of stone.

UNTITLED

Why does this abstract—
                    horizontal bands of black, magenta
and aquamarine emerging from

                    a wash of ocher—
make me think of watching sunrise
                    at Kill Devil Hills, it must be

three years ago? The past comes back
                    with the hazy clarity of Rothko's lines.
A soothe of cold sand my bare feet sink into

                    turns gold with the first hard light,
surf breaks along the shore like a zipper
                    pulled up on a dress.

The three gradations of water become visible,
                    turquoise shallows deepening
to indigo and, one mile out, indelible black.

                    Finally the sunrise
she and I got up for in the dark,
                    a reef of red

along the horizon, a thin line of rose
                    applied like makeup to a closed eyelid,
and the half-pupil of the sun

rising from the ocean
to stare unwinkingly upon us
                until we have to look away.

Away from the diamond facets of the waves
                that flash sheet lightning
and back to land, back to boarded-up blind bungalows,

                back to the high-tide line,
a dead horseshoe crab, the black hymn
                of flies that rises from it,

and the chicken-scratch scripture of sandpipers' feet
                upon the smooth wet margin
the surf erases as it withdraws and hushes.

                But why do I need to name
what the painter leaves untitled? The mind is a fine sieve
                through which morning and evening

slip and are lost. Only the abstract remains.
                The litmus bands
of sky, ocean, and earth. The image without particulars.

                Hourglass. Woman. An outline drawn
with a stick in the sand to be washed away.
                We give up title to our lives.

Yet there persists this hunger for the concrete,
                for lovers on a breakwater
to toss stale bread to gulls and watch them

                catch the pieces midair,
for the man with a metal detector
                in search of coins

to keep on vacuuming all morning the miles
                of golden sand
and be undazzled by the ocean's spangles.

MASTER OF THE LARGE FOREHEADS

Looking at this Adoration,
Limoges enamel which burns
in its gold frame
with blues and greens purer than flames
from driftwood, I stare
at the Madonna, whose forehead
swells like a gourd
left too long on the vine.
My brother's face
looks back at me,
slightly gibbous,
a full moon waning.
The Madonna has my brother's
blank eyes and thick lips,
from which my mother still wipes
curds of oatmeal.

Master of the Large Foreheads,
master of the jeweled thistle,
master of the oxen
whose lowing does not lull
the Christ child to sleep,
my brother is a bird
learning to sing
after twenty-two years
of silence, his first stuttered words
not "Mama"
but "yellow bicycle."

Master of the velvet folds
in the wise man's cloak,

master of the stones in the road,
master of sunlight
settled like fine, twice-sifted flour
on the thousand leaves of the birch,
I don't know why you painted
your people with foreheads that bulge,
or gave them eyes that are one white dot of glaze,
or why they have no ears.
It is enough that they kneel
in the blue dust, extracted
from the oxides of cobalt,
in awe of this ordinary birth
and that they offer clods of dirt
as their gifts.
It is enough that my brother
pulls me by the arm and points
to objects whose names
have flown back to them.
"Look," he gargles,
"Yellow yellow
house car-door flower,"
naming on and on,
singing in his few syllables
the world into place around him
until everywhere he looks
it's yellow.

EVERYTHING WE WORE

I. Grief

Crouched by my mother's shut door,
ear pressed to the veneer,
I didn't understand the sound
lower than crying. It went on and on,
like two branches rubbing together
that wouldn't let me sleep.
Closing my eyes, I imagined
a cut-glass bottle
of tears on her dresser,
how she anointed her face with them,
dabbed them into the hidden places
behind her earlobes,
on the inside of her wrists.
Whenever I came close
I smelled how they had dried.
They stayed on the fur collars
in the hall closet.
I would bury my face
in her winter coat of Persian wool,
inhaling the dim smell
that was part of everything we wore.

II. My Brother Learns to Eat

At twenty-one, he's the pumpkin man
we made for Halloween:
head, a jack-o'-lantern,
body, an old shirt of mine
stuffed with leaves.
He has my face
in the funhouse mirror.
The mouth my mother spoon-feeds
stammers her lost name.

Again she shows him
how to wrap squat fingers
around the handle of the spoon
his godfather gave him,
its silver-plated monogram
worn through to tin.
He clenches it so hard
the knuckles turn white.
The spoon trembles
gobs of oatmeal
onto the oilcloth iris.
We all stop eating
to watch the spoon
find his mouth. We wait
for him to swallow without chewing,
for his Adam's apple to rise in his throat
like words he can almost say,
for his hand to keep moving in its broken
dance to the mouth forever.

III. Inventing Water

That drink of water from Uncle Salvo's windmill:
so cold it left me breathless
like morning air
when I had to go make sure
the calves hadn't frozen.
I wouldn't call it water.

Maybe it was the way Uncle Salvo dipped
his hand in wrist-deep,
so I saw it bigger than it really was.
Fingers like link sausages,
veins magnified,
flowing into the rusted trough
where the sows drank.

Maybe the chipped enamel pitcher
had something to do with it.
Taste of iron at the roots of my tongue.
Or how I tilted my head back
to gulp the sky.

I could see to the bottom
where a machine had stamped in tin:
1957 Patent Pending.
The whole day to be invented,
I stood there in the rising dust of the farmyard.
Water so clear the pitcher looked empty,
filled only with light.

IV. Counting Vertebrae

My brother stayed home.
His voice was a bell
that wouldn't ring.
I was always asking Why?
Why the ocean?
Why the grass?
He had no questions.
His mind went round and round.
He was the room
no one entered.

I had to hold his fingers
clumped around the crayon.
I had to draw our town
for him, trees like chimneys,
the roofs of mountains,
snowflakes floating
into the open hand of fields.

He laughed and laughed,
clapped hands,
shook his head,
whipping it back and forth.

Every night he slept with me,
got twisted in the sheets
so his head was my feet.
I left him cooing

next to the warm indentation
I had carved in the mattress.

When I go home
I'm given a different bed.
A locked room away
he chuckles at the waking trees.
I am still wrapped around him,
my knees asleep in the small of his back.

Pulling my castoff sweatshirt over his head,
I count the vertebrae:
spine like a fern.
When I come to socks and shoes,
his feet are blue stones
among handsewn flowers
on the throw rug.
I massage the blood back.
His flat feet walk on lilacs.

V. Blackout

Dad notched my height
on the slaughtering tree.
I grew five inches
from killing to killing,
fat as a razorback
on hominy.
Mom wouldn't watch
but sang the same hymn
above the whetstone smooth as skin,
coming for to carry me home.
Her voice honed me
until I too could cut
through the belly of a sow.
Arms elbow-deep
in the dark jewel box of the thorax,
I learned by touch:
the liver slippery as brook trout,
the heart bigger than Dad's fist
pounding the kitchen table.

The sun turned green.
Trees walked.
I saw the sky's ribs,
pasture painted with hog's blood.
For a moment Mom sang
through the throat of the sow,
from a place I could not see
and had only grazed with the tips of my fingers.

VI. Heliotrope

Among the huge dazed faces
of sunflowers, my brother squats
waving a dead stick
in time to the shadow dance
of leaves. "What?" and "How come?"
his only two phrases,
a rare bird's trill.
He keeps trying to pronounce
my name, but it's too big
for his mouth.

He will never leave
the crayon garden,
still the stick figure
I tried to cross out
and scribbled brown grass over.
He grew back.
Checking his pulse against mine,
I hear crickets hum in his wrist.
Two beats to my one.

I can't teach him pitch.
Singing his own cracked scale,
he is happy.
Keeps turning his face to the sun.

Why must he stay
in the half-lighted house
that I only visit?

We have different words for good-bye:
he rubs his unshaved face
against my smooth cheek,
leaves a rash that stings
when it is gone.

VII. My Father's Crucifix

I wear you around my neck,
thin man with handcarved ribs.
We're the same tree.
I was cut from the grain of your thighs
and sanded down.
The knots in my flesh
are birthmarks.
You were given to me tied hand and foot
with red ribbon in a black box.
I left you among the bric-a-brac of my top drawer,
took you out only on Easter,
unwrapped the tissue paper
to make sure you were alive.

When I could not feel your wooden pulse,
I panicked. I wanted to breathe
back into your mouth
the used air, put my fingers
in your painted wounds.
You wouldn't speak.

I can't throw you away.
I learn to wear you
next to the skin beneath my fisherman's sweater.
Under the broken ribbing of undyed wool
you chafe a red noose
along my clavicle.
You do not hear my heartbeat,
the knocking at the back door

I do not answer.
Through the magnifying glass
you become almost human.
Skin is flawed sandalwood.
Between the shoulder blades
and the mahogany cross:
a rough spot the chisel could not touch.
We are left unfinished
in the places where two woods join.

VIII. 20/20 Vision

Turning the compost, I stand
there again, my pitchfork forgotten,
blowing raw fingers,
stunned by the pinpricks of rain
turned to hail. How the sun kept shining
like a brass shotgun shell.
Again I am waving and shouting
to an uncle two acres of black beans away
who plows with his back to the rainbow.

When will he turn, kill the engine
for good, or let its breath run idle?
The eyes at the back of his head
can't see how the rainbow has doubled,
how the barn's gambrel roof is held
in this short embrace of light.
He does not hear the roosters
crow kyries, cry mercy every morning
from the chopping block, their crops
full of stones that need to be fed.

He goes on plowing a straight line
towards a razor-edge horizon.
By the time he returns
my hands will have lost their fingerprints.
I will walk without feet.
Even now, I must squint
to find him, black sty

in the sun's bloodshot iris.
The sky closes like an eyelid,
and I move surely into darkness.

SHORT MASS FOR MY GRANDFATHER

1. *Kyrie*

Kyrie, the roosters cry across his eight hundred acres.
I go over last year's balance sheets,
pages scrawled with his spiderweb numbers.
On the debit side, 50 lbs. soy seed,
a new combine, 3 truckloads manure.
On the credit side, months go by.

2. *Gloria*

I pick up the sledgehammer
in Grandfather's workshop,
its haft worn down by his hand,
and trace the grain of ash
free of knots. It wants
to swing down to the mute anvil
and beat glory from the piece
of rusted iron pipe
he'd always meant to straighten.
The sledge sings and clangs
goddamn, goddamn, goddamn—
I hear Grandfather again,
the blood turning his thumbnail
rainbow, then black.
Glory to the sledgehammer,
and to the anvil,
and to my grandfather's hand
pounding out anger for all
the twisted scrap iron
that didn't obey him.

3. Credo

I believe in milkweed,
its star seeds drifting down
into the red clay.
I believe in Grandfather's gangrene,
the bad blood thickening to sludge
and his left leg, which still felt pain
though burned clean in the hospital incinerator.
And I believe in his wooden leg, pecked at by roosters
while he threw them handfuls of grain.
And in what the bantams said,
spreading their brass wings,
my grandfather's laughter
as he chock-chocked back at them.

4. Sanctus

I couldn't call it holy.
Yesterday, I found the roan gelding
with a last meal of maggots in its belly,
knotted black ropes of intestines,
and heard the monotone of flies
the tail used to swish away.
I turned from the smell.

Next year, perhaps I'll come back
to the austerity of ribs,
their signature curving into the ground.
My grandfather and I

once galloped the gelding bareback,
our knees feeling the knock of its heart
as we slowed to a walk.

5. Benedictus

I used to play hide-and-seek among the whispering ears.
Again the scarecrow's music calls me back,
pie pans like cymbals tied to its wrists.
I bow down to the scarecrow
dressed in Grandfather's best shirt
worn through at the elbows.
Lord of Cornfields, Lord of Crows,
watch over us, your face
rained away. Embrace the wind
with wooden arms and stand still all winter,
broomstick for spine, while your creatures, the crows,
peck at your head.

GRANDMOTHER'S QUILTS

1. Broken Dishes

Choosing a casket for Grandfather,
Grandmother found the coffin
she wanted for herself,
lined with green velvet
embroidered with sprigs of dogwood.
"I can't wait," she said.
Even the undertaker grinned.

According to her will,
she wants to be buried, wrapped
in her favorite quilt:
scraps of her own Grandmother's wedding dress
pieced with old curtains, chamois cloth,
union suits, and flannel sheets—
all feather-stitched into the counterpane
beneath which she conceived six children.
It is the simplest of quilting patterns,
no center, the scraps cut into isosceles triangles,
each attached to another, four triangles
making a square, the colors asymmetric,
repeated ad infinitum
and called "Broken Dishes."

2. Sampler

Put the colors together,
crushed velvet next to denim:
Grandmother, Grandfather,

the summer dresses hangers wear all winter
slowdancing with their shadows
in the walk-in closet,
Christmas cactus that opens handfolded petals
while the snow sifts down
big as confetti in the ticker-tape parade,
persistent as the dust on the pianoforte
Grandmother used to play
before arthritis hushed her fingers—
they are all sewn together.
They are made one.
One with the rusted bucksaw
hung in Grandfather's shed,
harp whose single strand of sawtoothed music
won't cut cordwood anymore.
One with the pincushion
stuck with needles
like a Voodoo doll.
One with the thimble
and the darning egg,
a stone Grandfather found
worn smooth and round.

3. Alphabet

Block letters
held together with cross-stitches,
white on red squares
like the alphabet blocks
I buried with Grandmother's trowel

and watered for a week.
When they didn't sprout
I dug them up,
helter-skelter alphabet,
half the letters missing.

A is for the red ants
who lived in small volcanoes.
C the cowflops
that turned to dried leather.
D is dragonflies, blue needles stitching
the thistles of the back pasture,
mating, midair.
E the porcelain egg
the old hen sat on for a year.
F forbidden word
Grandmother tried to wash out
of my mouth with Ivory Soap,
but I hid it under my tongue,
monosyllable hard as her slap
dissolving like sugar.
H is hymns, hellfire, and hallelujahs
rising like incense
to the Tiffany Christ
who walked flat-footed
on the cloud-churned water
and always looked at me
no matter what pew I sat in.
O all the waterlogged words
I still have to look up
in the dictionary I threw

into the cowpond,
tired of homework:
opprobrium obsidian
obsequy octillion.
P is the games of pinochle
Grandmother still plays
with her senior-citizen children
and wins, a nickel a point,
holding the meld of the queens of spades
and jacks of diamonds,
sly as a schoolgirl,
smirking as she lays it down.
W is wasps
and their nests of papier-mâché
which are not to be knocked down
but are places of worship.
X is for the unknown,
for whatever imaginary number
will solve our lives,
for the child who knows
that God burns
in the candelabras of sumac
and must forget it
to grow older.
Y the baked yams,
the slow bubble
of their caramelized juices,
black blood in the roasting pan.
Z zero,
zygote of moon and sun,
egg yolk of everything.

KAATERSKILL FALLS

Love, our bodies
are spring runoff
hustling down
a thawed streambed
pouring over
bald boulders, riff
of white water
like fingers among
sixteenth notes,
descending scale
of rocks and ledges
down glissandos
of shallow pools
where shadowed trout
glint and are gone
in sunlight's sleight
of hand, always
the pull
of the falls below
urging us faster
over gravel runs
and moss-slick slides
of washerboard granite
until we swirl
hurdy-gurdy
and spill over
the lip, a single
syllable
the falls croons
to itself, half crash
half hush, endlessly

lullabying
us down stairs
of sheer air
to where the water
shatters and raises
a fine mist
wrung from rocks
one hundred feet
below, down where
the falls wears
only a rainbow's
drizzle dazzle
see-through rags,
and the pool's applause
is as a ceaseless
xylophone
whose keys are the still
stones.

MY HIGH SCHOOL'S ROLL OF HONOR
FOR ITS WAR DEAD

1.

During study hall, I recited
their names under my breath,
William Butler de Rham,
Jonathan Burton Morehouse,
and the last one I could hardly pronounce,
Raphael Yglesias:
meaningless litany
carved on the oak scrolls.
They were a way to make time pass
when I wasn't watching the tendrils
of my friend's blond hair,
wet from the shower after practice,
drip onto the golden triangle of Pythagoras.
His numbers ran together.
I scratched my initials on the scarred desk
under the graffito of a woman
whose breasts were knots in the soft pine.

2.

Ten years later, I come back. It's spring break
and I walk down empty hallways
hung with the same Impressionists
in new frames. Gauguin's Tahitian girl smiles
and offers me mangoes from a tray
held just below the aureoles of nipples.
My scuffed shoes echo through the schoolroom.
I find our two desks sanded clean,

revarnished to a tabula rasa,
waiting for more names, more lust.
Above me, the roll of honor for the war dead
has grown, my friend's name spelled wrong.

3.

His face blurs more from year to year,
the line of his jaw smudged and half-erased
in the charcoal drawing I never finished.
He wouldn't sit still, said I was wasting an afternoon
we could have spent swimming in the reservoir.
We had to crawl through the hole under the rusted link fence,
cheeks scraping rough leaves of burdock.
Half the afternoon we floated on our backs—
a foot below us, the spring-fed cold
that didn't warm up even in mid-August.
When we swam back, it numbed our skin, testicles shrunk
to the size of plum pits.
No towels, we stretched naked
for the sun to dry us. When he fell asleep
I watched the way his breath
slowed and deepened, the arc of each rib
precise as a theorem from Pythagoras,
his body that I hadn't known I wanted to touch until now.

Remember, Lord, those whose job is to hold the support plate to the existing
column with vise grips and to turn their heads away from the welding rod,
shutting their eyes against its tail of sparks, which burn the wrist with a
pattern like chicken pox.

Remember the iron filings from the rotary grinder, how they mix with sweat and
run in at the corners of the mouth.

Remember Curtiss, who sands slag from the weld with a power wire-brush. How
the muscles and veins stand out on his forearm as if someone had sculpted
them, not the fifty hours a week plus overtime with Carolina Steel since he
turned fifteen and lied about his age.

How he signs his paychecks with an X crooked as a bad weld.

And Lehma, who boasts in a Tennessee drawl that he can make love with a forklift.
Who eases from the flatbed onto pallets on the ground two I-beams at a
time, each three tons and thirty feet long, balanced on the two prongs of the
lift. Who, like a tightrope walker with a balance beam, hardly breathes as he
shifts gears.

Remember the weak back of the foreman, who tells his crew to unload eight tons
of steel deck from the flatbed by hand;

And the electric hoist, which can lift up to five tons, which takes two men to work,
which they ride for kicks, crouched in the wire cage, twirling around and
around as it lifts them up the four stories of the hoist well;

And how they left Johnny D., the half-idiot riveter, kicking the chicken wire and
screaming for two hours to let him down.

Remember the thick straps reinforced with steel threads, which tie around the
girders and attach to the hook of the electric hoist.

Remember the bulletin board in the break room, stuck with thumbtacks. Its only
announcement: We hire without discriminating on the basis of color, creed,
sex, age, or ethnic origin.

Remember Floyd, fruit picker turned welder when the orchards closed, who tells
during lunch break of his eighteen-month-old son, born with red hair plas-
tered into a whorl on the back of his head, and how the skin over the fontanel
shone through like the ripe peaches he used to pick. How his son can already
say "steel" and "wrench."

Remember them and their children.

THE GIDEON BIBLE

I read what page to turn to
in time of loneliness
in time of sorrow
and in time of suffering.
Someone has underlined
a passage in blue pencil:
Be not forgetful
to entertain strangers
for thereby some have entertained angels
unawares.
I wonder what angels
have passed through this room,
have broken the cellophane wrappers
around the plastic cups,
rinsed the day's taste from their mouths,
and lain down on this bed
sagging from our thousand bodies.
Did they open the thin curtain
and try to find Orion,
the Dipper, and the Water Bearer
while the neon sign blinked off and on
WELCOME VACANCY?

God of the Scorpion and the Archer,
I'd like to love strangers,
your angels with all their aliases
stapled to post-office bulletin boards.

I'd like to believe
in your messengers who travel with no luggage,

who hitchhike to towns I've never heard of
and tell me they're going my way.

God of the centrifuge,
of interstellar winds,
and of each particle of dust
in the drifting nebulae,
your name is written
in the stitches of stars,
in the slow unraveling of the Milky Way.
You do not come down to us.
Or if you do, you come
not in our own likeness
but in the form of the cold morning mist
settling like fine sweat on my face and hands
when I open the sliding door
and step out on the balcony.
You are the sound of the traffic
that has somewhere to get to,
heading south along I-95,
traffic that mixes with the sound of surf a long way off.
I have nowhere to get to.
I count the slow pulse
of the red warning light
on a radio tower:
thirty beats to each minute,
hesitatingly steady,
fading as the day comes.

ALONG AN ABANDONED SPUR
OF THE C&O LINE

What I took for trash,
scraps of rags thrown
into the new grass,
its sparks struck from the stones
between rotting crossties,
turns out to be morning glories
twined over the iron rails.
Is it failing sight
and twenty-nine years of living in one body
that make me mistake
these angels come down
in the flesh of white
five-sided trumpet flowers?

Holding a blossom
in my palm, bringing it close
so I see the anthers sticky
with pollen, why do I remember
the skin of a doe
like pussy willows
as she lay on the broken yellow line
of Route 7, and the thud
a man's workboots made
kicking her in the belly
while she tried
to get up? How he
kept cursing her,
in words I hadn't learned yet,
for denting his fender?

I don't know why we can't endure
beauty. In my palm calloused
from eight hours a day of sledgehammer
and cold chisel, gutting houses
for Safeway Construction Co.,
the morning glory weighs next to nothing.
It's a white moth
lighted on my skin,
the brush of its wings
like a woman blowing
where she has licked
the inside of my wrist.

HOW NIGHT COMES

First we lose our shadows
walking together into the veiled fields
of shade tobacco.
Mountains are farther away,
the farmhouses whiter,
last light clotting their weathered boards.
Moon is a knothole in the grain of the sky.
Cottonwood fluff floats down to us,
the Milky Way going to seed.

We lose track of our feet
and have to go by touch alone,
warm dirt between my crooked toes.
Your fingertips are minnows
nibbling the collarbone.
Haystacks soften.
We are losing the plowed fields,
the road winding straight
into the alfalfa.
We are walking on the voices of crickets.
I touch the scars on your forehead
that darkness heals,
our bodies made whole again.
They have their own light.
We lie down in a drying shed
among cut sheaths of green tobacco,
their smell humid and close.
Putting your rough tongue
in my ear, you whisper to the night
around us like a halo
to take you slow.

APRIL'S ALGEBRA

Dunce cap of paper stars
April's fool
I figure the square root of rain
plus sun minus moon
times blackbirds times slingshot stones
a thousand times trillium
divided by the first bloodroot
to hammer up through the half-inch of humus
times thrust times ache
the seeds in the groin
times Mary Lou Melody Melissa May Johnson
twenty springs and the sprung backseat
of the Impala that's rusting in some back pasture
times the shy pigeons
that built their nest
in her Sears & Roebuck bra
and her size-10 feet
the petals of her painted toenails
times the double S's
of tire marks I laid down for her
on back roads
the stop signs I ran
and the moth-haloed streetlights
times Goldberg and Son's five
and dime times redbud
times the signs that said FILL DIRT/ROCK WANTED
and NIGHTCRAWLERS SOLD & TRADED
times skinnydipping in moonlight
that silverplated our acne-broken faces
the peepers shrilling the only vowel they knew
bass strings of bullfrogs

and the fiddlehead ferns
unfolding their question marks.
Divide it all by the dirt's itch for weeds
and factor the menstrual month
into burdock and crocus
brambles and binomials of jonquils
sprung from the mother lode of manure
I helped spread on the flower beds last fall,
everything raised to the power of everything,
and what do I get
but the decimals of grass
going on and on as far as the field goes
and beyond, the crazy circuitry of forsythia,
sparks from their crossed wires,
the pulse of tulip bulbs,
their blossoms' daily systole and diastole,
my heart murmur's stammer and stop,
the blood shuffling along on schedule,
bees mumbling in the azaleas,
always the same word repeated over and over.

ALONG MAGNOLIA ST.

The days are deciduous.
                        They keep falling,
dead leaves
                the wind blows
down the street
                        and scatters, or heaps
into windrows,
                which I walk through
kicking the leaves
                        so they crackle and spark
under my shoes.

                        I breathe in
their dark
                invisible smoke,
thirty-two years.
                        I remember
so little,
                a few faces
flickering past
                        in a tunnel,
going the opposite
                        way, to whom
I keep waving.
                Last stop
Magnolia St.,
                        the conductor calls
and I get off,
                a child, still

clutching the hem
                    of Father's coat.
He has to stop
                    and wait
at each landing
                    of the long stairs
that lead out
                    of the black mouth
of the subway
                    into the sudden
sunlight.

                    As we walk home
together, I take
                    two giant steps
to his one. Careful
                    not to walk
on the sidewalk's cracks,
                    I count the blocks,
wanting the street
                    never to dead-end
but go on forever
                    past all the signs
I can't read
                    but which Dad
spells out for me,
                    Bob's Auto Body
and the Atlas
                    Universal

Tool & Die Works,
                    past the litter
blown against
                    chain-link fences,
past the graffiti
                    of dogwood blossoms
that spring scrawls
                    against the grime
of a brick wall.

                    Today's dead leaves
spiral down
                    into puddles
which, with the scum
                    of oil slick,
become
            kaleidoscopes.
Wind soothes
                    the pavement
with rain
                    and whispers
through the half-
                    bare branches
that the past
                    is always
under my feet,
                    that it is never
lost, how if only
                    I stoop down

and listen closely,

          my father will speak

through an oracle

          of water

gurgling in the gutter

          and tell me how

to walk straight

          down these darkening streets

paved with rain

          and wet leaves.

HIGH FIDELITY

Special Bonus: Early Opera Singers Digitally Remastered,
          says the *High Fidelity* ad,
so that Caruso sings as if this year were

          1904 and it's encore
after encore in Milan, "E lucevan le stelle"
          bringing the house down

with those haunted, oboe-throated B-flats through which he climbs
          two octaves to love.
I listen to the voices of the dead, to what they leave

          unsaid, to Glenn Gould
humming as he plays the *Goldberg Variations* if you turn
          the volume up,

an almost inaudible accompaniment, a gruff
          basso profundo
to the glitter of arpeggios as they glide like schools of minnows

          from his fingers.
The dead are greatly gifted. They have a kind of glamor
          the living don't enjoy,

the glamor of being done with it. We listen
          to their voices
recorded in mono on scratchy 78's

          played back
in digitally remastered sound, with Dolby to reduce
          the background hiss,

brought "back to life." Dennis Brain, changeless now,
           who will never run out of breath,
his each slur of embouchure flawed and perfect in Brahms's

           Horn Trio in E-flat
broadcast live in February 1957, half a year
           before he drove

his favorite sports car head-on into a tree.
           Like him, the living
move through their lives faster than the speed of sound,

           vanishing before
their voices reach us. Or, like Callas, they outlive
           the legend of their voices.

And what of that failed Irish tenor turned poet,
           the drag queen of us all
who lip-synched a washerwoman's brogue

           and double-dubbed his aria
to Anna Livia Plurabelle for an early
           version of the gramophone?

O, he's hiding underground with stem and stone,
           amen, and won't come out
again. What of his friend, the madman Pound

           who shouted his sestina
in praise of war to the sound of drums like grumbling thunder
           to shock a London

literary salon, *enfant terrible* who broadcast
            on Rome Radio
his harangues between selections from Vivaldi

           and, listening to the playbacks,
found his own voice "strange"? What of our American mezzo,
           not Marilyn Horne

but Miss Bishop, unbeliever who loved to sing the old hymns,
           "A Mighty Fortress
Is Our God," as well as her own Brazilian

           carnival zarzuelas,
her "Pink Dog" doggerel, in uninflected cantankerous
           Yankee? Their voices

outlast them, slipped from death's dark sleeve, wiped
           free of dust,
spinning around and around

           on the turntable. And what
voiceprint shall we leave behind us in our turn?
           To whom do we

broadcast? Are we the fabled radio tower of Babel,
           our voices wandering
all the lost wavelengths from zero to one

           thousand megahertz
heard at once? White noise for the deaf soul,
           Mozart's last

piano concerto for a virtuoso with no hands.
What shall we leave on the voice-activated
recorder in the black box of the poem?

Small talk,
a bad joke, "five thousand fucking feet and falling"?
Glenn Gould hums

to those slow variations on the one theme
that gradually accelerates,
gets rephrased, played upside down and backwards,

and arrives
at the beginning, which is the same but different.
Pray that our fingers

may have faith in the score's almost imperceptible
changes of key,
its syncopations, rests, slurs, appoggiaturas,

and that we
may hum in an undertone to harmonies only the mind hears.
Pray our voices,

though they break, may carry in "high fidelity"
which, as the dictionary says,
is sound reproduction over the full range of audible

frequencies
with little distortion of the original signal.
Listen to the dead.

ZION CANYON, EASTER SUNDAY

At six o'clock in the fading dark
my father and I are climbing Angels Landing up the switchback path,
one side rock wall, the other

a sheer drop three hundred feet into the North Fork Virgin River,
a steel-gray ribbon
that still reflects the full moon sunk low in the sky.

My father has to stop
and rest at every other bend, and I do some quick
arithmetic to figure out

that he'll turn seventy-five this June.
Maybe it's the gray
morning light, or the insomnia keeping him awake from midnight

until four every morning,
that has washed all color from his skin. He hasn't shaven, and his face
is grizzled with stubble's

hoarfrost. Under his chin the flesh hangs in loose folds.
I once caught a tree toad
with the same pendulous jowls and held it in my palm, so frightened

it didn't hop away.
It sat still while I watched the heartbeat jump in its throat.
Where is the man

with whom I paddled thousands of miles in a canoe, Lake Champlain,
the Allagash, Au Sable,
Hudson, Richelieu, St. Lawrence? We even canoed through New York City

                    past the Pallisades,
       the Bronx and the projects, past Ellis Island, the East River
                    and the Statue of Liberty

until the Coast Guard sent a speedboat after us. How disappointed
                    they were when we told them we didn't
need them. I ask my father if he remembers going down

                    the Housatonic in late November
with snow on the ground, and how after portaging around a tree
                    fallen across the river,

he stepped into the bow, carrying my brother on his back,
                    while I held the stern.
The canoe flipped. My father trod water with my brother,

                    who couldn't swim,
clinging round his neck so hard he could barely breathe or splutter
                    Help! as he held out

his hand to me, perched on the trunk of the tree. When I couldn't reach him,
                    I jumped after a moment's
hesitation into the cold November river to drown with them.

                    He says he'll never forget
me jumping in, or how he swam against the current back to the bank
                    with my brother, or having to dive

to pull me out. A hundred yards further, he sits down
                    on a boulder and tells me
to go on without him—"I'll just stay here for a while

and then turn back.
You'll catch up with me on the way down." I ask him what
about watching the sun

rise, as we'd planned, over The Great White Throne. "I'll see it
well enough from here."
It is the grayness in his face, and how his voice blurs the syllables,

that makes me nod,
turn back to the trail, and keep climbing until first light touches
the west rim of the canyon,

a single gold streak igniting the shadows into red rock,
revealing the striations
of the stone that it took millennia to erode into Tabernacle Dome

and Court of the Patriarchs.
What I know cannot be written down either in gold letters by the fiery
finger of God

or with the stub of a blunt pencil in words I keep erasing.
The only vision I have
on the switchback trail to the top of Angels Landing

is of me and my father
canoeing a blaze of water past Isle La Motte to where Lake Champlain
narrows at Rouses Point:

how we crossed over the border against a head wind into Canada
and had to pass through customs,
a one-room hut on the end of a dock, to which we tied up

so a sun-wizened septuagenarian
who hadn't seen anyone on the river for the last three days
could ask us the old

cataclysmic questions, "Where are you going? What is your place
of birth? How much
currency are you carrying? How long will you stay? When will you return?"

LIFE CLASS

1.

After half a lifetime of life classes
I've ended up as the unknown model
in Philip Evergood's *Nude by the El*,
1934, oil.
I lie back on my plush red sofa
with its scroll arms
and rejoice in cacophonous colors,
in the clash of the indigo Persian carpet
with the lipstick-colored upholstery.
The painting is a tacky valentine
to the ordinariness of nakedness,
to the asymmetry of my breasts,
one nipple pouting, the other unaroused.
It's a valentine to my big, ungainly
beautiful feet, to the Sixth Avenue El seen
through three floor-to-ceiling windows
as it disgorges its rush-hour passengers
onto an empty platform.
It's a valentine to all the palpable improbable
congruities, a real girl
lolling naked against a background
of screeching wheels, girders, and the third rail
while commuters ride backwards on the rapid transit
and read what the Dow Jones closed at,
unaware of the rising percentage points
of my bare breasts
and of the volume traded that day
on love's bull market.

I am the center of it,
though everyone in the picture
looks away from my nakedness.
Juju, the artist's wife, drinking coffee
in the lower right-hand corner,
next to his signature,
is there, fully clothed, to keep an eye on the men
who've chipped in to buy this afternoon with me,
two dollars fifty cents an hour,
in the sun-flooded studio.

The man holding his palette and dirty brushes
like a bouquet of flowers
has a muscle shirt but thin arms
and looks out the window
smoking his pipe nonstop.
Evergood's blond friend
sketches quickly and sees only
what he draws.
Behind me, the gilt-edged mirror reflects
a pink door and the frame of the easel
on which this canvas rests.

The room smells of mineral spirits,
Evergood's gin-and-tonic,
my cheap perfume, the men's sweat.
Dust motes float their gold notes
down the stave of a shaft of sunlight.

Another local crashes past.
I fight the urge to go to the window and wave

at the crowd of commuters
with their black felt fedoras
and plastic-flowered sun hats,
to yell at them until they look up
the four stories of this brownstone,
to remind them of what they have forgotten
among memos, stock quotes, and deeds of trust,
how under the silk dresses and sharkskin suits
are the brutal beatitudes
of their own bodies.

2.

For my eighth birthday,
Mother gave me my first dance classes.
Those hours at the barre
have become years—pliés, grands battements,
battements frappés, ronds de jambe en l'air,
clockwise, counterclockwise, more turn-out,
the voice of the dance master
shaping our bodies into prima ballerinas'
while the piano player played Satie's
Gymnopédie. Sex was everywhere,
in the stale smell of sweat and lavender perfume,
in the steamed-over windows,
in the séance-like knockings of hot-water pipes and radiators,
in the crumpled pastel pointe shoes
and piles of towels and leg warmers
thrown off like molted skins,
from which my body has risen

to finish with feet in fifth position
and bras en lyre.

3.

Why do I always lose my name
when I kick off my high heels,
pull this madras dress over my head,
and step out of a silk slip
into my own fine skin?
In their charcoal drawings,
oil paintings, cutouts, marble busts
and plaster casts,
I am Woman with Black Stockings,
Reclining Figure, Odalisque,
Girl before a Mirror,
Sunbather, Torso,
Bathsheba at Her Bath, Nude Negress,
or Venus of Voluptuousness.

This is not anatomy class.
I am more than a collection of bones
held together with tendons,
more than clavicle, ilium, sacrum, pubis,
femur, tibia, fibula,
Latin names that sound like a tune
played on a xylophone.

As the Grand Inquisitor said to Paolo Veronese
who argued that nakedness was unbecoming

in a painting of Christ and his saints,
"Do you not know
that in these figures by Michelangelo
there is nothing that is not spiritual?"
Non vi è cosa se non de spirito.
The body is not different from the soul.
The curve of the buttocks
in the red-chalk *Study for Libyan Sibyl*
expresses God as surely as the purest
Latin plainsong of a choirboy
in the Sistine Chapel.

Everything there is,
my two breasts smooth as wet clay
under the potter's hands,
the nipples beginning to harden into unripe kumquats,
the tongue that sucks me
until I shiver like a Chinese gong
when it's struck,
is of the spirit.

4.

But I am alone, a nude without a name
in a life class. Holding the same pose
for an hour, rigor mortis already setting in,
I will not be a caryatid
keeping my back straight
for two and a half thousand years
along with my sisters

who hold up the acanthus-carved
cornices of some civilization
whose roof has fallen in.

No thanks, honey.
When I shimmy out of my camisole,
I don't want people to reach
for stone and a chisel.

Shifting from one leg to another,
I wonder what the nameless nudes
in the atmosphere-controlled rooms
of all the world's museums
were thinking while they held
their cramped, lifelike poses.
How to pay the rent?
Who will sharpen
the emperor's javelins?

5.

The only one I know
with a name
is Hendrickje Stoffels,
Rembrandt's live-in mistress
who turns away sadly
from the artist who refuses
to marry her, but sees
out the corner of her eye
how he daubs another unsalable

Old Testament painting.
Her body is thickening
at the waist.
The foreshortened perspective
makes her left hand
huge and clumsy.

She is supposed to be
Bathsheba at her toilet.
A household crone
washes her feet,
then gives her a pedicure.
King David's letter,
dangling from her right hand,
sends condolences
on her husband's untimely death
and requests that she consider
his offer.

What does a widow
say to the king
who has gotten her with child?

Her whole grieving body asks
from the still-firm breasts
to each toenail's inlaid
mother-of-pearl.
The wise old crone
keeps massaging her feet
and is silent
in the golden shadows.

Is this crumpled piece of paper
really an old love letter
from Rembrandt,
which she has read and folded
so many times that it is nearly
worn through at the creases?

Or is it a greasy grocery list
used as a studio prop:
onions new potatoes
leeks cream peppercorns
3 lbs. ham hocks?

Or is the sheet
blank, waiting for each of us
to pencil in our own spent lives
on this paper held
in the model's warm, ungraspable hand?

PSALM FOR THE SUMMER SOLSTICE

If this life's the only text we have
        and each day's a page
of longhand, a rough draft of transubstantiating clouds

        that change from odalisque
to sine curve to pineapple to cotton batting
        to kinks of uncarded wool

and then to nothing but the blank blue
        of mindless heaven
without ever finding the one exact

        monosyllable to describe
what our anonymous millionth-millennium B.C.
        author originally intended,

then I'd like to bequeath this poem as one more
        endnote to infinity.
Let it be a variorum of all the voluminous

        pages of new leaves
printed with light. Let me annotate the scrolls
        of surf unrolling

on the beach where my wife and I walk, eating raspberry
        Italian ices
in paper cones, our tongues lolling along the sheer

        delicious deliquescence
of this the longest day before it all dissolves
        to the spittle's

tingle in the pink dark of our throats. Dull tongue stained
    a telltale indelible
flamingo, let me whistle off-key and watch for hours

    the ocean
dash its signature of foam and flotsam
    along the high-tide line.

Tangled twine, driftwood, tarred dolls, and condoms
    swollen with saltwater seed
all spell desire and the burgeon of oblivion.

    Nine months pregnant,
my wife must stop for breath. She puts my hand
    on her belly taut

as a spinnaker ballooning with the first gust of wind
    so I may feel
again the kicks and shadow punches of our child snorkeling

    in the warm salt water
of the womb's horseshoe harbor. We tell time differently
    in the ninth month.

Our clock is the child knocking on the door of her cervix.
    Her blood moves
to the tide's timetable—rip, neap, flood, and ebb. She has passed

    through the phases
of the moon from first quarter to full, and still to come
    birth's partial

eclipse. We are at zero's zenith. Everyone
               is celebrating
the long hours of sunlight by flying kites,

                 letting the string
slip through their fingers as the wind takes their lures
               and lofts them,

parti-colored constructions of paper thinner than skin
               with pine sticks
for bones, some in the shape of snakes or dragons

                 or pterodactyls,
competing with the screaming gulls. They strut the air and pantomime
               in peacock feathers,

gliding and bowing to the pavane of wind that thrums
               through the umbilical
of lightweight twine down to the hands of children who feel

                 each trill
and tremolo travel along their arms. Cut the lines loose. Let the kites
               hover forever

on the updraft of this poem, I want to say. No words can salvage
               the day in all its dazzle,
the rhinestones that the surf throws at our feet, the ocean

               like crumpled tinfoil
spread out flat on a table. The children will reel their kites in
               with nothing on the line

but their bright bait. Are words no more than kites whose long tails
          troll the sky
for invisible bluefish with scales like tarnished silver,

          which we will never
land, though we feel their pull? Thirty thousand feet
          above sea level,

the jets leave their vapor trails, chalk marks the wind erases
          with one slow hand.
Here, on the beach, sunbathers cast in bronze

          doze or listen to the latest
crooner's love song, the extended weather forecast, a news update
          on more terrorist bombings

in Beirut, while a one-prop plane flying low along the surf
          pulls a streamer of huge cutout letters
that proclaim SAM'S CLAMS, ALL U CAN EAT RESTAURANT & HAPPY HOUR!

          Fifteen minutes later,
it returns flying the opposite way with its sign now backwards,
          !ЯUOH YԀԀAH

and TИAЯUATƧЯ, words in a lost language that I repeat
          to savor their revved-up *R*'s
and roll of gutturals, which make me think of the Aramaic

          Mene, Mene, Tekel, Upharsin.
This is the day that the Lord our God hath made
          and numbered

in all its contradictory glory, where a man and a woman
                    stand on the fulcrum
of the year and are not yet weighed in the balance

                    that finds the world
wanting. In her womb our child waits to come kicking
                    into the blinding

searchlight of sunlight, to add its own wails to the sum
                    of all the other
cries, which are the only praise there is.

WELCOME HARDINGS' CLOCKS & MUSIC BOXES

When I walk in, the grandfather clocks are chiming at odd
                    unsynchronized intervals.
With all their various tick-tockings, it's like listening

              to a hundred leaky faucets fill
their porcelain washbasins until they spill over on the hour
              in a cascade of cable-wound

triple chimes. Each clock tells a different time, and I feel
                    like Einstein, or the March Hare
dipping his friend's stopped pocket watch in a cup of tea.

              Time doesn't matter
to the Mad Hatter & Co. It's easy to kill an hour or two
                    and forget my afternoon

appointment in this room where all times are more or less true.
                    "Tempus fugit,"
reads the motto on a pinch-waist grandfather clock

              whose brass lyre pendulum
hypnotizes me for a moment so I see my mother warning me
                    not to procrastinate

over problems in long division or fractions,
              which I haven't mastered
yet, or ever—my mother turned overnight from the girl

              in her wedding picture,
spit curls and a sassy don't-you-dare-kiss-me pout of a mouth,
                    to a seventy-year-old

woman with one breast left. Her face is crackle-glaze porcelain
                    late Ming Dynasty.
"Don't worry," she says. "Everything always turns out for the best."

                    A cuckoo clock chimes
from the wall. Its four Tyrolean hand-painted peasants,
                    two miniature couples,

revolve to a snatch of a waltz as the cuckoo comes out
                    of her nest and nods
to each chime. Under their bell jars, the anniversary clocks

                    maintain the monotonous
back and forth of their four brass balls. "They used to be wound
                    once a year

and were unreliable," the shop owner tells me. "Now, of course,
                    they're quartz
and never need winding." They're guaranteed to last a lifetime,

                    never *to quiver*
out of Decimals—into Degreeless Noon— To think that the delicate
                    intermeshings of cogwheels

in the Swiss works of a gilded rococo cuckoo clock by Bulova,
                    with a tolerance
of a few micromillimeters, will outlast my mother

                    and, probably, me
is ridiculous, and comforting. The hour hand will keep creeping
                    over the dial

of days, on which, although we do not see it,
        the snow melting off
a roof will trickle and tick down into a waterfall

        of icicles
honed to the cold blue fire of unclouded diamond.
        Everything will continue,

almost the same. The sky with its cumulus Rorschachs.
        The trampled confetti
of dogwood petals scattered on the sidewalk after the rain's

        parade goes past,
twirling its batons of lightning. All the ecstasies
        of spray paint

on the railway trestle, I LOVE JACK
        or MARY GIVES GOOD HEAD,
which the highway department paints over once a year.

        Even the music boxes
which I wind to hear the thirty-six-note rolls of "Für Elise,"
        "Memory,"

or Pachelbel's Canon in D will keep playing their sentimental
        tunes. The porcelain
ballerina pirouettes on her pedestal to the strains

        of "Clair de Lune"
while around and around go the wooden riderless horses
        of a candy-cane-striped

carousel to "Love me tender, love me true" inside
                    a glass ball
which I shake to make it snow. Such kitsch is wonderfully

                incorrigible. All the different
melodies crisscross to the counterpoint of a hundred clocks
                    ticking and chiming.

What a weird cacophony I get, so artificial it's almost
                    natural.
A man with a bright orange hunter's cap comes into the shop

                to pick up his mother's
grandfather clock, which her ex-husband shot "in the face" with a .33
                    because she liked it.

The owner has repaired the works and straightened out the minute
                    hand, but the bullet hole
is still there between three and four o'clock.

                "She didn't want it
fixed completely. She wanted the story." That's it!
                We want the story

of what we can't keep, and we want to smile a little
                while we embellish it for
whoever will listen, strangers, nobody, ourselves.

                The shop owner
starts telling me about the one-armed clockmaker who taught him
                how to take apart

a watch and put it back together blindfold, who plays
                   every Sunday
the church organ, Bach preludes he's rearranged for one hand

                 so no one hears
his missing arm. I tell him I want to write a poem about his shop.
             "Whoever likes my shop

likes me," he says. "Send me a copy when you're done."
             I tell him he'll be waiting
years. As I go out the door, I see the sign I didn't notice

               when I came in:
Welcome Hardings' Clocks & Music Boxes. Outside, it's alternating
              rain and sleet. Welcome,

I say to myself. Welcome rain. Welcome mud. Welcome the dead grass
              and unopened
crocus buds under slushy March snow. Welcome coming in and welcome going out.